PRAYING WITH CHILDREN

Some Ways and Means

Jenny Pate
DIOCESE OF LANCASTER

Illustrated by Paula Knock

McCrimmons
Great Wakering   Essex

First published in Great Britain in 1995 by
MCCRIMMON PUBLISHING CO. LTD.
10-12 High Street Great Wakering Essex SS3 0EQ
Telephone (01702) 218956 Fax (01702) 216082

ISBN 0 85597 546 6

ACKOWLEDGEMENTS

HARPERCOLLINS RELIGIOUS PUBLISHING DIVISION, 77-85 Fulham Palace Road, Hammersmith, London W6
8JB, for extracts from *Welcome!* by Jenny Pate and *Listen!* by A.J. McCallen.
KEVIN MAYHEW LTD, Rattlesden, Bury St Edmunds, Suffolk IP30 0SZ, for the chorus and verses 1, 3 and
5 of *Do not be afraid* © 1978, and for verse 4 of *My God loves me*. Reproduced by permission, licence
no. 599091.
SR OSWIN MARSH SCHJ, 203 Bristol Road, Birmingham B5 7UB, for the extract from *The world was in
darkness*, taken from *Let God's Children Sing*, first published in 1968 by Geoffrey Chapman (a division
of Cassell plc).

All the songs used in this publication can be found in *The Complete Celebration Hymnal*, *Celebration
Hymnal for Everyone* and *A Year of Celebration*. All published by McCrimmon Publishing Co. Ltd.

Illustrations by Paula Knock
Cover design and text page layout by Nick Snode
Printed by BPC Wheatons Ltd, Exeter, Devon
Text printed on Fineblade 90gsm, cover printed on Invercote 240gsm
Repro by Anagram Litho Ltd, Southend-on-Sea, Essex

Contents

Preface

'Ignorance of the Scriptures is ignorance of Christ' – as St Jerome said and the Second Vatican Council repeated (Dei Verbum 25). A bishop looks to his schools to impart a real knowledge of and friendship with the person of Jesus. That is why the principal textbook of a school is the Bible. 'Therefore let the Christian faithful go gladly to the sacred text, whether in the sacred liturgy ... or in devout reading, or in such suitable exercises and various other helps which ... are happily spreading everywhere in our day. Let them remember that Prayer should accompany the reading of Sacred Scripture, so that a dialogue takes place between God and man. For "we speak to him when we pray; we listen to him when we read his Word" (St Ambrose)' (Dei Verbum 25).

I commend this book which attempts to put these words of the Magisterium of the Church into practice. It can be used in school, in the home and in those precious children's liturgies at Sunday Mass. Everything in it has been tried, tested and highly appreciated!

✠ *John Brewer*
BISHOP OF LANCASTER

Planning prayer with children

Introduction

When praying with children aim to:

○ keep to small groups, with the smallest range of age possible, it helps to personalise the experience and offers greater scope;

○ keep it short, keep it moving, children's attention span for any one activity, lasts approximately one minute per year of the child's age *(ie. five year olds can be reasonably expected to actively participate in worship for about five minutes; ten year olds, ten minutes);*

○ keep it simple and uncluttered;

○ start with something that draws everyone together, then move to a deeper understanding of the theme and conclude with a response;

○ create a place for prayer and worship *(even if it's only a table/cupboard top, corner or under the stairs).*

Include a variety of experiences such as:

stories / ritual / silence

prayer (children's own and traditional) / songs

sharing food / movement / music

dialogue / readings, from scripture (and other sources)

poems / holding/shaking hands / artefacts

sayings

Involve children in planning the worship, for example for older children:

Prepare five boxes

in box one put a selection of readings

in box two, a selection of songs, pieces of music

in box three, a selection of activities such as, giving, receiving, making chains, mime, drinking, dancing …
(write each activity on a separate card)

in box four, a selection of suggested visuals such as, statues, pictures, photographs, flowers, greeting cards …
(again write each suggestion on a separate card or on the actual visuals to be used)

in box five, a selection of prayers, traditional and children's own.

Invite a group of children, about five, to

- choose a theme for prayer

- choose one card only from three boxes

- plan an act of worship.

They may need to return to the boxes, discourage them from having too many elements. If group after group repeat the same reading or activity or song, remove the card for a while. Introduce planning only when they have had sufficient experience of praying. The themes on the following may help to trigger some ideas.

For younger children

Prepare theme boxes, such as Advent, holy days and holidays, school days, birthdays ...
In each box put a selection of appropriate pictures, songs, artefacts, readings; whatever might aid prayer, let the children choose.

NOTES

For ease of use the paragraphs in this book have been designated a style, according to who is speaking:

General narrative	– Roman	No indent
Spoken by teacher	– **Bold italic**	No indent
Prayers and songs	– *Italic*	Indented
Bible texts	– **Bold italic**	Indented

Candles

A theme for dark, wet days

You will need lots of candles, of all shapes, sizes and colours; some matches and taped music.

GATHER

Dim the room and gather the children around a table with a single candle.
Invite the children to think of one word which describes how they feel looking at the candle glow. After about a minute ask them to say their word (in turn) aloud, stressing that it does not matter if they repeat each others' word.

Blow the candle out. Ask the children to think of one word which describes how they feel now. When they have had sufficient time to think, ask them to say their word (in turn) aloud.

Re-light the candle saying these or similar words,
'This is Jesus, Light of the World, who came to bring ...'
(repeat the words the children used to describe the candle glow).

FOCUS

Become aware of the company of Jesus, symbolised by the lit candle.

Invite the children, in the privacy of their own minds, to talk to Jesus about whatever they wish.

Turn on the taped music and spend a few minutes enjoying his company and the candle glow.

CELEBRATE

The children in turn, place around the single candle, lots of other candles, every shape and size. As each candle is lit and placed on the table they state their prayer intention, concluding with,
'Lord in your mercy,'
to which everyone replies,
'Hear our prayer'.

To vary this prayer liturgy, use guided prayer of imagination as the Focus.

Be still

A theme for winter

You will need, a table covered with a deep blue cloth, a large white candle placed in the centre and a printed sign saying 'Be Still'; some matches and taped music. The children will need to have collected some items that represent stillness to them, such as stones, shells, twigs etc.

GATHER

Turn on the taped music.

Gather around the table quietly, one at a time place each child's still item on the table.
Sit and look at the items.
Invite them to make themselves as still as the items on the table.

We can appear to be as still as these things, at least on the outside but we can't be that still inside. Blood and oxygen are rushing around our bodies. Thoughts and feelings are too.

FOCUS

Turn on the taped music, very low. Read aloud the following sentences, *pausing* after each.

What thoughts and feelings are rushing around your body?

What's on your mind today?

Catch your thoughts/feelings.

Imagine a table in front of you.

Put your thoughts/feelings on the table.

Imagine that Jesus is sitting next to you at this table.

Talk to him about what is on the table.

Long pause

What does he say to you?

Long pause

Open your eyes.

CELEBRATE

Sing –

> *Be still and know that I am God,*
> *be still and know that I am God,*
> *be still and know that I am God.*
>
> *I am the Lord that healeth thee,*
>   (repeat 3 times)
>
> *In thee, O Lord, I put my trust,*
>   (repeat 3 times)

Words: Anonymous

📖 Celebration Hymnal for Everyone no.71

Love

A theme for February or whenever ...

You will need, some packets of 'Love Hearts' sweets, a copy of St Paul's letter 1st Corinthians 13: 4–7 'Love is ...' and the words and music of the hymn, 'My God loves me'.

GATHER

Give out the 'love heart' sweets. Tell the children to sort them into two groups, those which really speak about love and those which are silly and do not. When they have finished, ask for the number of sweets in each group and ask them to explain one or two choices. Gather up the sweets.
Ask, *'What is love?'*

FOCUS

St Paul tells us; ...
Read 1st Corinthians 13: 4–7.
If the language is too difficult for
the age group try the simplified
version below.

> *Love is always patient and kind*
> *it is never jealous or a show off*
> *it is never rude*
> *it doesn't remember hurtful deeds.*
> *Love is happy where there is truth*
> *it is always ready*
> > *to say good*
> > *to trust others*
> > *to hope*
> *and to stand by people in*
> > *good times and bad.*

Pause

Reflection –
(read by a different voice)

> *God our Father loves us,*
> > *He is patient, kind,*
> > *sees the good in us and*
> > *forgets the wrong that we do,*
> *He trusts us and*
> > *has great hopes for us,*
> *He will stand by us*
> > *in good times and bad.*

CELEBRATE

Sing –

> *My God loves me,*
> > *his love will never end.*
> *He rests within my heart*
> > *for my God loves me.*

> *My God loves me,*
> > *his faithful love endures,*
> *and I will live like a child*
> > *held in love secure.*

Words: verse 1 anonymous,
verse 4 Sandra Joan Billington

📖 A Year of Celebration no.149
📖 Celebration Hymnal for Everyone no.499

Give the 'Love Hearts' away to
loving children and adults.

Inside – outside

A theme for any time of year

You will need, four or five parcels, at least one should be elaborately wrapped and one in a used carrier bag. In the elaborately wrapped parcel place a fairly uninteresting gift and a very interesting gift, (perhaps the latest craze) in the carrier bag. Put whatever you wish in the other parcels.

GATHER

Display the parcels on a table. Gather the children around the table.
After they have had time to study the display, ask the children to choose a parcel and to indicate their choice by raising their hands as you lift each parcel in turn.

Open each in turn, leaving the best (ie. the carrier bag) until last.

Point out that this is how we sometimes judge people. We judge them by their outside appearance. We know very little about them inside. It is often the way we choose friends.

FOCUS

A story told by Jesus

Luke 18: 9-14, retold

'Two men went to the Temple to pray,' Jesus said. 'One was a strict religious man whom everyone looked up to.
The other was a cheat whom everyone disliked.

The religious man was proud. He prayed like this: "I do thank you God, that I am better than other people. I go without food twice a week and give away a lot of my money. I am not a cheat like that man over there."

The cheat, stood much further away, with his head bowed, too scared to look up. He said, "God, have mercy on me, I am a sinner." '

Who do you think pleased God?

Jesus told everyone listening to the story that it was the cheat.

CELEBRATE

God is concerned with what is in our hearts, what we are like inside. He does not judge us by how we appear on the outside.

We praise and thank you for your story O Lord.

Let us pray –

For the times we have chosen our friends by how they look on the outside:

We are sorry Lord.

For the times we have pretended to be good:

We are sorry Lord.

For the times we have laughed at people, called them names because of the way they look on the outside:

We are sorry Lord.

God our Father,
You made us in your image.
Help us to see the good inside ourselves, and in others.

Don't let us be fooled by outside appearances.
Help us to really get to know each other.

Amen.

Mary

A theme for May or whenever you like

You will need, lots of pictures of Mary (created by the children, perhaps illustrating the mysteries of the Rosary as well as professionally produced pictures or artefacts) and some flowers. You will also need some taped music.

GATHER

Whilst the taped music is playing, the children pin up or arrange their pictures and artefacts.

FOCUS

Spend some time looking at the display, choose a favourite picture or artefact and enjoy

looking at it. Tell them to close their eyes and imagine climbing into the picture or sitting by the statue.
Let the scene come alive and spend a few moments joining in.

After a few minutes begin the litany.

Mary, mother of Jesus,	**Pray for us**
Mary so happy,	**Pray for us**
Mary so sad,	**Pray for us**
Mary so patient,	**Pray for us**
Mary so worried,	**Pray for us**
Mary so hopeful,	**Pray for us**
Mary so tired,	**Pray for us**
Mary so busy,	**Pray for us**
Mary so puzzled,	**Pray for us**
Mary so excited,	**Pray for us**
Mary so wonderful,	**Pray for us**
Mary, Queen of Heaven,	**Pray for us**

CELEBRATE

One at a time, the children place flowers around the display, while everyone sings.

Sing – '*As I kneel before you*' or some other song to Mary.

📖 The Complete Celebration Hymnal no.401

Kingdom spotting

A theme for anytime

Before you begin take the children on a walk, preferably in a busy area. Tell the children to look out for people doing good, for example, someone comforting a crying baby or standing back to let someone else pass. Tell them to make either a mental note or to put it down on paper.

When you return:

GATHER

Gather together singing,

Seek ye first the Kingdom of God, and his righteousness, and all these things shall be added unto you; allelu, alleluia.

Alleluia, alleluia, alleluia, allelu, alleluia.

Words: Karen Lafferty

📖 Celebration Hymnal for Everyone no.633

FOCUS

Say together –

> **Our Father who art in heaven,
>   hallowed be thy name.**

Each child in turn, stands and announces the good deed they saw. After *each* announcement, respond.

Response: *girls only*
> **Thy kingdom come,
>   thy will be done.**

Response: *boys only*
> **On earth as it is in heaven.**

CELEBRATE

Say together –

> **Our Father, who art in heaven,
>   hallowed be thy name.
> Thy kingdom come.
> Thy will be done on earth as it
>   is in heaven.
> Give us this day our daily
>   bread,
> and forgive us our trespasses,
> as we forgive those who
> trespass against us.
> And lead us not into
> temptation, but deliver us
> from evil.**

Sing –

> *Rejoice in the Lord always,
> and again I say rejoice.*   (4)

Words: from Scripture

📖 A Year of Celebration no.52
📖 Celebration Hymnal for Everyone no.617

Go in peace to love and serve the Lord!

Praying for each other

A theme for anytime

You will need a blanket and lots of space!

GATHER

Gather in the school hall or some other large space. Tell the children to run about the hall, using all the space and avoiding bumping into each other.

After a few moments, tell the children to crouch down in their own space, hiding their eyes.

FOCUS

Throw the blanket over one child, be sure to cover them completely.

Tell the other children to gather around the child covered with

the blanket. Ask them to work out who it might be by noticing who is missing (this may contribute towards their sense of class/group/community).

Reveal who is under the blanket.

The children all lay their hands on this child and say,
God bless (N) ... and keep you safe from all harm.

Repeat this process, focusing on as many children as you feel appropriate.

CELEBRATE

Gather in one large circle, holding hands say a favourite group prayer or sing a favourite hymn.

The time to pray

A theme for life's turning points

You will need a clock face.

GATHER

Gather the children together just before midday. Ask them, *'When is the best time to pray?'* They may suggest times, occasions, situations, all answers are correct.

Show them the clock face, set at midnight/midday.

'Does midnight belong to yesterday or today?'
'Can the midnight moment be found?'

'Does midday belong to the morning or the afternoon?'
'Can the midday moment be found?'

Midnight is a moment when we leave one day behind and begin a new one.
When the midday moment comes, we leave the morning behind and begin the afternoon.

There are many times in our lives when we move from one thing to another. They are good times to pray.

FOCUS

Prepare the children for a moment's silence.
Let us all stand for the midday moment.
Pause for a moment of silence, then just before midday say

> *Leave all the problems and mistakes of the morning to God's mercy.*
> *Leave God's love to look after this midday moment.*
> *Leave this afternoon to God's care (providence).*
> *Amen.*

CELEBRATE

At this turning point of the day, turn to Mary (or say some other collective prayer):

> *Hail Mary, full of grace,*
> *the Lord is with thee.*
> *Blessed art thou among women,*
> *and blessed is the fruit of thy womb, Jesus.*
> *Holy Mary, Mother of God,*
> *pray for us sinners*
> *now and at the hour of our death.*
> *Amen.*

> *I leave the past to your mercy.*
> *I give this moment to your love.*
> *I put my future into your hands.*

A prayer walk

A theme for a summer's day

GATHER

Take the children on a walk (or to an interesting place).

During the first walk tell the children to concentrate on what they can hear; on the second walk, what they can smell, on the third what they can feel, on the fourth what they can see.

Make a note of their observations.

FOCUS

Sit in a circle, name your observations in turn, after each saying …

> *We thank you Lord, we praise you Lord!*

CELEBRATE

Sing – *'The clapping Gloria'!*

📖 A Year of Celebration no.181
📖 Celebration Hymnal for Everyone no.408

Colours

A theme for Autumn or whenever you choose

You will need a large bowl filled with water and some floating candles of various colours (the kind that can be bought in craft shops and department stores).

GATHER

Pause for thought,

What colour comes to mind when you think of Monday?

What colour comes to mind when you think of Friday?

What colour is happiness?

What colour is sadness?

What colour is hope?

What colour is tomorrow? ... yesterday?

Young children will have difficulty thinking in colour. Ask for their favourite colour and use 'favourite' as a theme for prayer.

FOCUS

Ask the children to choose one colour (from among the floating candles) and to say what that colour brings to mind. Make that the prayer intention.

Light the candle and while it floats say your prayer.

or

Choose a colour eg. red. Ask, **'is this a happy or sad colour?'** If the answer is happy, ask the children **'What makes you happy?'**

Light the candle and while it is floating the children in turn say what makes them happy.

Everyone responds to each child with,
> **Praise the Lord** or **Glory to God in the Highest.**

What gives you hope:
> *Our hope is in God our Father*

What makes you sad:
> *In good times and bad we can trust God.*

CELEBRATE

Sing – '*Colours of Day*' or some other song appropriate to your theme.

📖 A Year of Celebration no.78
📖 Celebration Hymnal for Everyone no.118

Do not be afraid

A theme for anytime

You will need some buttons, stones, shells or leaves.

GATHER

Gather the children into groups of about five. Give each group a bag of buttons/shells/leaves, whatever you have chosen. Include enough ie. one per child and two or three extra.

Ask the children to pass the bag around the group, each taking one button out.

Tell the children to examine the button carefully, get to know it well. When they are sure that they would recognise it anywhere, put it back into the bag.

The bag is once again passed around the group. Each child retrieves their button.

In retrieving their button they will use the word 'mine'. It will be used many times. Listen for it, encourage them to use it by picking up buttons and asking, 'Whose is this?'

Point out that everyone used the word 'mine'. Tell them to hold on tight to their button, whilst they listen to the reading.

FOCUS

Jesus said
'You are mine
I know each one of you
I will never forget you or lose you.
We will be together for ever.

God my Father has asked me to
take care of you
because you belong to us.

No-one can ever take you away
from us.'

Adapted from John 10:27-30 and
Welcome! by Jenny Pate

CELEBRATE

Sing –

Do not be afraid   (Chorus)
    for I have redeemed you.
I have called you by your name;
    you are mine.

1 *When you walk through the*
    waters, I'll be with you.
   You will never sink beneath the
    waves.

3 *When the fear of loneliness is*
    looming,
   then remember I am at your
    side.

5 *You are mine, O my child; I am*
    your Father,
   and I love you with a perfect
    love.

Words: Gerald Markland

📖 Celebration Hymnal for Everyone no.147

Tell the children to keep tight hold of their button. It will remind them not to be afraid.

Precious things

A theme for anytime

You will need each participant to bring a precious item. Children will confuse precious with expensive, you will need to make the distinction clear, perhaps by describing an item that is precious to you. You will also need a table covered with a cloth and a cup (chalice) and plate (paten) hidden from view.

GATHER

Begin by explaining why the item you have brought is precious to you. When you have finished place to object on the table.

Each child in turn does the same.

After everyone has finished look at the table, which by now will look pretty cluttered. Point out that any stranger walking into the room might imagine that a jumble sale was about the start. Not having heard our stories they could never know just how important these items are to us.

FOCUS

Bring into view the plate (paten*) and using the words below or similar explain its significance.

THE PLATE HOLDS BREAD:
Bread for us is ordinary stuff, we eat it every day. It is very tasty and satisfying, when we break it we make a mess.

Sometimes we use bread as a nickname for money. We know what it is like to be blessed with money to spend and we know what it is like to be broke and have no money to spend.
We know what it is like to be blessed with friends, we also know what it is like to break with friends and to be unhappy.

The bread in the paten becomes blessed and broken. It is a sign of all the blessings and broken moments in our lives.

Bring into view the cup (chalice*)

THE CUP HOLDS WINE:
Wine is often drunk on special occasions such as weddings and funerals. It is drunk during happy times and it is drunk during sad times.

The wine in the chalice is a sign of all our hopes and fears, happiness and sadness.

Through this wine Jesus tells us that he is with us in all our dreams and disappointments.

Place the chalice and the paten on the table.

Pause for thought

CELEBRATE

Explain that in churches such items are kept in special places. They are cared for in a special way to show that they are not ordinary. To show that we value our precious things we can make a holy table/shrine/special place.

Ask the children to prepare a holy table/shrine.

'What would you want to display. How would you show it was special?'

When the shrine is completed, gather around it and sing a song.

Sing – *'In Bread we bring you Lord'*, by Kevin Nichols.

📖 Celebration Hymnal for Everyone no.302

* If the chalice and paten are inappropriate for the age group you are praying with, introduce some other artefact such as a statue.

Use your shrine as a focus for prayer, changing some of the items from time to time to reflect the theme.

Telling tales

A theme celebrating forgiveness

You will need a candle, a bucket of sand, some slips of paper and some pencils.

GATHER

Play some music to quieten the children.

Ask them to close their eyes and try to remember a time when someone told a tale about them, which resulted in them feeling very embarrassed. Give them plenty of time to think.

After a few minutes, invite them to share their experiences.

FOCUS

One day Jesus was busy teaching in the Temple.
A group of people came in bringing a woman with them. They made her stand up in front of everybody and everybody looked at her.
They said to Jesus, 'This woman has been doing bad things, the rules say that she should be stoned as her punishment. What do you think? (They really wanted to put Jesus on the spot.)
Jesus bent down and started to write with his finger, then he looked up and said, 'If there is anyone among you who have never done anything bad, then they can throw the first stone'. Then Jesus bent down to write again.
One by one they went away. Jesus said to the woman, 'Has anyone thrown a stone at you?' She said, 'No'.
Then Jesus said 'Neither will I, you are forgiven, go home and try to be good'.

Adapted from John 8: 1-11
Taken from Welcome! by Jenny Pate

We do not know what Jesus wrote on the ground. What do you think it might be?

Take care not to confuse what Jesus wrote with what they are going to write/draw.

CELEBRATE

What do you think Jesus thought of the 'tell tales'?

He will always forgive us. He is gentle. Our confession does not have to public. He will forgive us in private.

Give out the slips of paper, ask the children to think of something they wished they had not done and to write/draw it on the paper. Tell them to fold the paper. Invite them to approach the candle and set the paper alight, then drop it into the bucket of sand to finish burning. As each piece of paper is lit, everyone says,

Jesus you take away the sins of the world, have mercy on us.

All together –
Oh my God because you are so good, I am sorry that I have sinned. With your help, I will try to be good.

Everyone matters

A theme for anytime

You will need a small vase of flowers per group. Simple flowers such as daisies, dandelions, forget-me-nots, etc.

If this is taking place in school, you will need a list of children's names and their absences.

GATHER

Ask the children to look at the flowers and choose one that is a little like them, one that they can identify with for whatever reason.

Pluck one out and ask,
'Does the vase of flowers look as good?'
Pluck out a few more, pointing out that as you do the vase of flowers becomes less interesting.

Tell the children, it is just like that when any of them are missing from class/away from home. They are missed!

FOCUS

A reading to think about.

Taken from Listen! by A. J. McCallen.

> *One day Jesus said:*
> *'Look at the flowers!*
> *They don't worry about anything, and yet they look more beautiful than a King dressed in his best clothes!*
>
> *So don't worry about yourselves. If God takes so much trouble over the flowers even though they are going to be cut down tomorrow and burnt, then he will certainly take good care of you'.*
>
> *From the Gospel of Matthew*

CELEBRATE

We missed the flowers when they were taken out of the vase. But not as much as we missed you!

Name the absent children and the dates of their absence.

After each all say,
> *'We missed you ...'*

Make cards for the absent.

Disaster

A theme for times of disaster such as famine, flood, plane crash, etc

You will need newspaper cuttings of photographs, headlines and as many crucifixes that you can find.

GATHER

Read out some of the headlines, show some of the photographs.

At a time such as this many people ask, 'Why did God let it happen?' They say that God should stop such disasters. 'Where was God?' they cry.

Look at the photographs again. Point to one of the victims.

That is where God is!

Remember Jesus, God the Son, he showed us where God is, he is with us. His life wasn't so easy. Yes, he was strong and made good things happen but he was also weak and often hurt. Remember how he died.

God isn't only with the powerful, he is also with the weak. It may seem as though he is a thousand miles away but he is really very near.

FOCUS

We may feel this problem is too much for us. What difference can we make?
There is a famous prayer:

> I am only one
> but I am one
> I cannot do everything
> but I can do something.
> What I can do,
> I ought to do
> I will do,
> by the grace of God.

Pass the crucifixes around the group, as each child receives the cross invite them to pause and say, *'Lord Jesus I will help the weak.'*

CELEBRATE

Create a focal point to remind you of the people affected by this tragedy.
Plan some response such as, fund raising, sending cards, writing letters, etc.

Sing – *'Make me a channel of your peace'*
📖 A Year of Celebration no.147
📖 Celebration Hymnal for Everyone no.478

or *'God's Spirit is in my heart'*
📖 A Year of Celebration no.44
📖 Celebration Hymnal for Everyone no.227

or *'In the land there is a hunger'*
📖 Celebration Hymnal for Everyone no.307

I wonder

A theme for anytime

GATHER

Gather the children in a quiet, comfortable and private place.

Ask the children, *'What do you wonder about?'*
Give them plenty of time to think and gather their thoughts, some children may like to draw a picture.

Invite them to say what they wonder about.

Everyone sits and listens in silent respect. When they have finished you may like to list single words, which name or describe what they are wondering about in some way.

FOCUS

Some people came to Jesus to ask lots of questions.
They wanted to know what happens when we die.
'Do we still have the same relations?'
Jesus said, 'When we get to heaven we will all be together and all our questions will be answered.'

Adapted from Luke 20: 27-28

CELEBRATE

Display the children's pictures

Say together –

I praise you, Lord,
and I am filled with wonder.
For everything you do
is strange and marvellous.

Say or sing a Gloria, perhaps some other song of praise such as:

Rise and shine and give God the
glory, glory.
Rise and shine and give God the
glory, glory.
Rise and shine and give God the
glory, glory.
Children of the Lord.

Words: Traditional

📖 A Year of Celebration no.173

44

Remembering people who have died

A theme for November or anytime

You will need a candle, some matches and a bowl of holy water.

GATHER

Gather the children around the Paschal candle and the holy water. Explain that this special Easter candle is lit at a funeral. It is a sign that when we die our life changes, it doesn't end, it changes, just like Jesus' life did at Easter.

Holy water is sprinkled over the coffin as another sign that the dead person's life has changed (*not* ended).

FOCUS

A letter from St Paul.

Taken from Listen! by A. J. McCallen

Dear Friends,
I want to tell you something
about people who die,
because I don't want you to be
terribly sad
like other people are,
for we are Christians!
We know that Jesus died just as
we do,
but then he went to live with his
Father in heaven.

We will do the same.
We will go to live with God our
Father for ever.

I am certain of this,
because Jesus said it was true.

CELEBRATE

Invite the children, in turn, to move towards the holy water font, to name someone who has died, to dip their finger in the water and make the sign of the cross, remembering that the person they mourn is enjoying a life changed not ended.

When everyone has finished, pray together.

God our Father,
we pray for our friends and
relations who have died.
They are living with you now
and getting to know you more
and more.
We know they are very happy.
Give them our love, we miss them
but we look forward to the day
when we shall be with them and
you in heaven.
Amen.

Poppies

A theme for peace

You will need lots of poppies.

GATHER

Invite the children to hold up or
look at a poppy.
Ask the children if they know
what the poppy symbolises and
why?

Poppies covered the killing fields
of the First World War as a
result of the bombing and
fighting. The poppy seed has a
hard shell that needs to break
to germinate. The violence and
vibrations of the fighting helped
to break the seeds.
The red field poppy is a frail
flower. If picked, it quickly dies.
It grows in the poorest of

conditions, at roadsides and where the soil is thinnest.
Yet this flower has the loudest voice. It is worn every year.
It cries PEACE!

FOCUS

Peace is Jesus' Easter message.

*Later on, on the same day that the friends had discovered the empty tomb,
they locked themselves in because they thought the soldiers might come looking for them.*

*During the evening Jesus came into the room and said,
'Peace be with you.'
The Friends were really pleased! Jesus said again, 'Peace be with you.'*

Taken from Welcome! by Jenny Pate

CELEBRATE

Leader: *For all children troubled by war.*

All: **Peace be with you.**
(If you have poppies hold them up)

Leader: *For all children who are teased or tormented.*

All: **Peace be with you.**

Leader: *For all children involved in a family argument.*

All: **Peace be with you.**

*Jesus came into the world to bring peace. He wants us as his followers to spread peace throughout the world.
Let us start now by offering each other a sign of peace.*

Not yet

A theme for Advent

You will need a table displaying bare twigs, planted bulbs showing no sign of life and any other items that may symbolise 'not yet'.

GATHER

Gather around the table, spend some time looking at the items displayed.

Take a close look at (for example) the bare twigs. You may think that it is impossible for those twigs to grow. Inside them is everything they need to grow. But not yet, the right time has not yet come, they have to wait.

What would you like to be able to do but can't yet?

Pause, give the children the opportunity to share their thoughts with God in silent prayer.

Advent is a 'not yet' time.
There are many 'not yet' moments
in life. Can you think of any?

FOCUS

*For many years, people waited
for God to send a saviour.
When the time was right, he did!*

Here is a letter from St Paul

> *Dear Friends,
> When the right time came,
> God the Father sent Jesus to us.*
>
> *Jesus had a mother just like the
> rest of us
> and he had to do as he was told
> – like us.*
>
> *He wanted to help us all,
> and he came to give us the chance
> to become the 'Children of God',
> so that we could call God 'our
> Father' like him.*

Listen! A. J. McCallen

CELEBRATE

Divide into two groups.

Group One
> *I dreamed the world was all
> stretched out in front of me,
> but now it was made new.
> I saw the city where the
> people lived,
> but now it seemed like part of
> heaven.*

Everyone
> **LORD** *I* **PUT MY TRUST IN YOU.**

Group Two
> *I heard a loud voice and it said,
> 'God has come to live with his
> people!
> He has made his home with
> them.
> They will be his chosen ones.
> He will be their loving God.*

Everyone
> **LORD** *I* **PUT MY TRUST IN YOU.**

Group One
> *'He will wipe away the tears
> from their eyes.
> He will put an end to suffering.
> There will be no more of this
> sadness.
> There will be no more of all
> this crying.*

**There will be no more of all
this pain.
Trust God.'**

Everyone
LORD I PUT MY TRUST IN YOU.

Adapted from Praise!

Sing –

*The world was in darkness
and nobody knew
the way to the Father
as you and I do.
They needed a light
that would show them the way;
and the great light shone
on Christmas Day.*

*From Let God's Children Sing,
by Sr Mary Oswin*

ALTERNATIVE SONGS

'*City of God*'
📖 A Year of Celebration no.113
📖 Celebration Hymnal for Everyone no.65

'*Majesty*'
📖 Celebration Hymnal for Everyone no.477

'*Come and join the celebration*'
📖 A Year of Celebration no.61

Christmas

You will need, younger children to prepare a Christmas tree bauble around which is the baby name band that was wrapped around their ankles in the maternity hospital.
Older children might like to write their full address, which goes on to include, the world, the universe, etc.
You will also need a crib.

GATHER

Ask some of the older children to read their address, starting with the last line.

Point out that God's creation is huge (He is still creating!).
He loves all his creation. But he loved the world so much that he had to join in.
He knew that meant joining in the bad times as well as the good.

FOCUS

Ask some children to place Mary, Joseph and Jesus in the crib.

St John tells us,

God is not living in heaven far away from us.

God is born.

He is living with us. His name is Jesus.

John 1: 1-18

CELEBRATE

When God joined the world, he was born as a baby, just like us!

While everyone sings, the younger children hang their Christmas bauble (with the baby band), on the Christmas tree.

You may like to add some other artefacts associated with babyhood around the tree/crib, a potty even!

Sing – '*Away in a manger*'

📖 A Year of Celebration no.58
📖 Celebration Hymnal for Everyone no.66

Other resource books from McCrimmons for school use

PRAYER BOOKS
Reference

A New Catholic Prayer Book   / includes prayers, bible texts and the Mass   0 85597 477 X
Gospel Prayers   / prayers inspired by the Gospels   0 85597 511 3
Some Catholic Prayers   / including: The Hail Mary – I Confess – The Rosary   0 85597 483 4

HYMN BOOKS
A Year of Celebration   / 198 pieces
    Melody/guitar edition   0 85597 544 X
    Pupil (words) edition   0 85597 552 0
Celebration Hymnal for Everyone   / 856 pieces   *(Various editions and bindings)*
The Complete Celebration Hymnal   / 827 hymns   *(Various editions and bindings)*

ASSEMBLIES
Assemblies for Infants   / assembly themes   0 85597 442 7
Signposts   / assembly themes for years 3 to 7   0 85597 443 5

OTHER BOOKS
Liturgy of the Word for Children   / 50 schemes for Sunday Masses   0 85597 387 0
More Liturgies of the Word for Children   / schemes for Sunday Masses   0 85597 426 5
My First Communion Book   / a guide through the Mass for children   0 85597 370 6
Praise God   / a Mass book for children   0 85597 530 X
What Christians Believe   / includes: The Creed, Sacraments, Commandments   0 85597 481 8
What Jesus Taught   / includes: The Beatitudes, Our Father, Some Parables   0 85597 482 6

CLIP ART COMPUTER DISCS
Clip Art for Little People – Volume 1   / 150 greyscale & line images   *(PC-DOS or Apple Mac)*
Clip Art for Little People – Volume 2   / 150 greyscale & line images   *(PC-DOS or Apple Mac)*